THIS BEAUTIFUL WORLD   VOL. 26

LAPLAND

by VALERIE STALDER

Published by
KODANSHA INTERNATIONAL LTD.
Tokyo, Japan & Palo Alto, Calif., U.S.A.

Distributed in the British Commonwealth (excluding Canada and the Far East) by Ward Lock & Company Ltd., London and Sydney; in Continental Europe by Boxerbooks, Inc., Zurich; and in the Far East by Japan Publications Trading Co., C.P.O. Box 722, Tokyo. Published by Kodansha International Ltd., 2–12–21 Otowa, Bunkyo-ku, Tokyo 112, Japan and Kodansha International/USA, Ltd., 599 College Avenue, Palo Alto, California 94306. Copyright © in Japan 1971, by Kodansha International Ltd. All rights reserved. Printed in Japan.
LCC 70–158638
SBN 87011–153–1
JBC No. 0326–783019–2361

First edition, 1971

CONTENTS

THE JOURNEY

I shall never forget the first Lapp I ever set eyes on. I was standing in a snow-covered clearing when he made his sudden appearance, and his brilliant clothes—of the brightest blues, reds, and yellows—held me spellbound. What a vivid splash of color he made against the wide, white landscape! What an unbelievable contrast to his surroundings! I had to remind myself that he was a living, contemporary representative of the most ancient nomadic tribes of Europe.

He came toward us, toward my Norwegian friend and me, walking jerkily as his body shifted from side to side with the rather bandy-legged gait that (I later found out) is characteristic of many Lapps. A few feet away from us he paused and surveyed us (it seemed to me) somewhat mistrustfully. Then, at last, he said in a slow voice, *Buris—buris baeve*. It was a standard Lapp greeting, much the same as "Good day," and I was pleased to hear it, for he was to be our guide on a sledge trip into the land of the Lapps.

Within a moment or two I realized that all other clothing from now on was going to look drab by comparison, and I thought how tremendously exciting it was going to be to explore this country and to meet its people, especially if they all wore costumes as gorgeously colorful as his. A prickle of excitement ran down my spine as I realized that now I was truly in the Land of the Lapps.

Curiously enough, there is no single country named Lapland. It is, in fact, not a nation at all, but rather a geographical area comprising bits of four modern states—the northernmost parts of Norway, Sweden, Finland, and Russia. It extends from the northwestern coast of Norway to Russia's Kola Peninsula in the east, and from Norway's North Cape to as far south as Roros in Norway and the mountains of Storvaetteshaahna in Dalecarlia, Sweden (both of which lie at approximately 62°30′ N). This represents a region about 1,100 miles long and, tapering from north to south, 240 to 60 miles in width.

Although Lapland occupies a fairly large area, the Lapps themselves are not numerous. By far the majority—some 22,000—live in Norway; Sweden has about 10,000; Finland, about 2,500; and Russia, only 2,000. Of these, many have become Scandinavianized in a number of ways—some by intention, others through indifference. For one thing, many have stopped wearing their Lapp costumes—those costumes by means of which it was once possible to tell at a glance the tribe that a Lapp belonged to. Nowadays many Lapps take these clothes out only for such special occasions as weddings, and not always even then.

Anthropologists agree that the group that today can be considered the most typically Lapp are the reindeer breeders in the mountains at the extreme north of Norway and Sweden—broadly speaking, the area around Kautokeino, Karasjok, and Karesuando. Our guide was a man from Kautokeino, and this was the tribe on which I intended to concentrate first and foremost, for their ways of reindeer herding are the most interesting, and their costumes (which most members of the tribe wear the year round) are by far the most colorful. In short, the Kautokeino are the most authentic Lapps, the most steadfast in the traditions of their ancestors, and therefore the most rewarding to study.

When one tries to find out something about the origins of the Lapps, one finds oneself in the midst of a heated controversy, for their earliest ancestors are so obscure that even the most knowledgeable scholars cannot agree about who they were. The earliest known reference to them is by the Roman historian Tacitus, who wrote in A.D. 98, "I have heard rumors that, north of the wild Germanic tribes, there lives a still wilder people—the *Fenni*." The term is explained by the fact that the ancient, generally used Nordic name for the Lapps was *Finns*, whereas the Finns themselves were called *Kvaener*. In fact, Lapland was long ago known as Finnmark, and some of it is still called Finnmark to this day—the northernmost part of Norwegian Lapland, where Kautokeino is—although today's Finnmark is only about one-eighth the size of what it once was. The Finns themselves called this part of the world *Lappi*, which means "the remote, the northernmost lands," and during the Middle Ages this word spread to Sweden and then to the rest of Europe.

That explains the origin of the name Lapps, although even today, in remote parts of northern Norway, there are still people who call them Finns. But if we ask where those ancient Lapps came from, we find we are in very deep water indeed. Some authorities theorize that they were originally a Samoyed tribe that pushed its way westward; they point out, in support of this theory, that certain physical features are common to both Lapps and Samoyeds and that there are certain words common to the two languages and

LAPLAND 🦌

found in no others. A further point is that the Lapps in their own language call themselves *Samer*.

One scholar has advanced the theory that in the Ice Age, when large areas of Northern Europe were covered by enormous glaciers, the Lapps lived and hunted below the ice borders, migrating later through northern Russia.

Another suggestion is that during the Bronze Age the Lapps were scattered over a wide area from Finnmark down to the Baltic because, as a people who lived exclusively by hunting and fishing, they needed an enormous area to be able to exist. Indeed, it has been proven that in the year 1550, in a large region of some seven thousand square miles in West Finnmark, there were only 150 Lapps hunting and fishing. It is also certain that as the remote lands to the north became freed of ice the Lapps hunted the wild reindeer further and further north in Finnmark and also fished in the Arctic Ocean.

The wild reindeer was, of course, their most important quarry, for it supplied them with meat, milk, butter, and cheese, as well as with skins for clothing. And it was the wild reindeer that was to shape the Lapp way of life. At first there were so many animals that every Lapp hunter had more than enough for his needs; the best time for hunting was then late in the autumn, when the herds migrated north from summer pastures to winter forests. The fact that hunting was so easy, however, resulted in the tremendous thinning out of the herds.

Gradually the hunters of each region began to realize the dangers of decimating the herds in this way. The hunters themselves, of course, had to have reindeer meat and skins for survival, but they soon saw the need to protect the herds that returned regularly to *their* part of Lapland from hunters in other regions, where the reindeer roamed the rest of the year. And the way to do this, they reasoned—the way to protect the herds from other Lapps as well as from beasts of prey—was to follow the animals on their wanderings. Reindeer are compelled to keep moving, away from the heat of summer and back to the forests in winter, always searching for the lichen and grass they require. When the reindeer migrated, the hunters had to migrate too. Thus it was that the Lapps became nomads. The needs of the reindeer shaped the lives of the ancient Lapps just as they shape the lives of nomadic Lapps today.

Slowly the wild reindeer became accustomed to the presence of man, and before long the Lapps managed to capture some calves, to break them in, to train them to carry things and to pull sledges—in short, to make them into semidomestic animals.

But even before they began to migrate with the reindeer, the Lapps already appreciated the need to regulate and apportion both hunting and fishing rights. The Lapps living in one region, therefore, organized themselves into a protective group which they called a *sita*. This consisted of a number of families who shared all the rights to a certain area and who helped each other defend those rights against the encroachment of strangers. The members of a *sita* hunted all big game as a group (although they also hunted small game individually), and all special hunting gear belonged to the group as a whole. The *sita* also looked after members who fell ill and saw to it that no one was in want. It shared among its members benefits as well as tasks and responsibilities.

Thus, as the need to migrate became apparent, the members of each *sita* regularly migrated together and helped one another with the herding of the reindeer. They shared such duties as tending the animals, branding them with a special mark to distinguish them from other herds, rounding them up when necessary, breaking them in as draft animals, and, finally, slaughtering them to provide food and clothing. Among the true nomads of Kautokeino this *sita* system is still very much in evidence, and families that are closely related to each other still migrate as a group.

The Lapps were not the only people living in the far north of Europe. The Scandinavians too had been pushing further and further north over the centuries, establishing farms and other agricultural settlements, and as the centuries wore on, clashes between the two peoples became increasingly frequent.

Then some of the more powerful Scandinavian farmers found a way to undermine the Lapps: they forced them to pay tribute. One such farmer was a traveled man named Othere, who lived in Helgoland towards the end of the ninth century. In the course of his travels he went to England, where he gave an account of this tribute to no less a personnage than King Alfred the Great. He reported to the English monarch that of all Norwegians he, Othere, lived furthest north, that he owned cattle, horses, sheep, and pigs, but that the largest part of his income was derived from the tribute his men exacted from the Lapps—tribute comprising the skins of reindeer and other animals, bird down, walrus tusks, even whale and seal hides.

Each Lapp was required to contribute according to his ability. Better-off families, for example, had to pay fifteen marten skins, five reindeer skins, one bearskin, ten tubs of down, one coat fashioned of either otter or bear, and two ropes sixty yards long, one made from whale hide and one from seal skin.

Othere, and others like him, exacted this tribute not only from the Lapps who lived continuously in the region but also from the nomadic Lapps, who came only periodically. The Scandinavian farmers kept all of the tribute they exacted for themselves, not being required to turn any part of it over in the form of taxes.

This situation came to an end when the Scandinavian monarchs realized that Lapp tribute could be a benefit to the royal coffers. Norway's King Harald Fairhair sent a northern chieftain, with a hundred men, to trade with the Lapps and to collect taxes from them in the king's name. In Sweden also, other tax collectors were equally busy, trading with the Lapps and exacting tribute for the crown. Few in number and poorly organized, the Lapps were no match for these aggressive traders, avid for the riches of the wild forests—skins of marten, beaver, otter, bear, and squirrel, as well as down, meat, and fish.

Gradually, over the centuries, certain Scandinavian families came to acquire special rights to trade with the Lapps and collect taxes. This activity became, in fact, their means of livelihood. The most avaricious of these families were the so-called Bir-karls (originally farmers from Pirkkala in Finland), who settled in Lapland and formed a sort of trading company by means of which they divided among themselves everything the Lapps had to trade. As this activity continued over several centuries, some of the Bir-karls grew enormously rich—at the expense of the Lapps.

As late as 1358 the Swedish king confirmed officially that the Bir-karls were to retain their special privileges as traders and tax collectors among the Lapps. This arrangement did not come to an end until the sixteenth century, when King Gustav Vasa curtailed the royal grant, and the Lapps at last found themselves freed from the burden of being the bondsmen and property of the Bir-karls.

The long centuries of taxation and bondage, however, had not only had a drastic economic effect on the Lapp people but had also instilled in them a strong feeling of inferiority. What is more, even after they were freed of their bondage to the Birkarls, their burden of taxation was in no way lightened. On the contrary. Since, at that time, the borders between Norway and Sweden, between Sweden and Finland, and between Finland and Russia were not clearly delineated, the Lapps of the northernmost districts now found themselves paying taxes to all four countries. Even worse, they were frequently fined by the officials of one country for having paid taxes to another.

Few in number, distributed widely over enormous spaces, the Lapps have lived their lives under conditions of impoverishing extortion and political chaos. For all these reasons they have never succeeded in forming a state of their own. Although the place where they live is known to the world as Lapland, it has never become one land.

As we waited in the snowy clearing, our guide had been busy harnessing reindeer to the sledges—one to each. The only Lapps who use more than one reindeer to a sledge are those of the Kola Peninsula in Russia. These Lapps are nearer to the Samoyeds, from whom they acquired the practice of attaching three animals to each vehicle, but this usage is not in the genuine Lapp tradition and is unknown elsewhere in Lapland.

Customarily, a simple halter is put around the head of the reindeer; no bit is used, as it is with horses, for the reindeer will not tolerate it. The sledge is joined to the harness by a broad leather strap, often beautifully decorated, and the rig is completed by a single rein for directing the animal. While in motion, the driver keeps the rein on the right side of the animal; then, to bring the deer to a halt, he shifts the rein to the left.

We were joined by other members of the little expedition we had organized—several Norwegians who, for various reasons, wanted to travel with us from Karesuando (in Swedish Lapland) to Kautokeino (in Norwegian Lapland). The journey, which would be made entirely by reindeer-sledge, was to take us three days.

The sledges themselves were quite unlike what I had expected, being merely bare planks nailed together over a pair of runners, with a reindeer skin thrown over the boards and fastened by ropes. There was nothing to lean against at the back of the sledge and no protection over the top of it, but both these problems were, I discovered, capable of a fairly simple solution. First, the driver's rucksack was fastened to the end of the sledge to form a rough sort of back, and then a second reindeer skin was thrown over his legs. Later I learned that sledges of this type were originally intended for the transport of goods, not people, and that real driving sledges have a stern board to lean against.

There are, in fact, many kinds of sledges in use in Lapland, depending on the purpose for which they are employed. Some sledges are built-up at the sides; some are half-covered with hides nailed to the front to protect the driver from snow; others, intended for the transport of fragile or valuable goods, are completely covered. The precursor of all modern sledges was made entirely of reindeer hide, in which goods were wrapped for transport, while one of the oldest types of sledge, and one still occasionally seen today, is a hollowed log that looks almost like a half-finished canoe.

Our Lapp guide, Aslak Utsi, with the help of his sister Elsa, formed a caravan of the sledges, one behind the other, by tying each halter to the back of the sledge in front. Aslak placed Elsa at the tail of the caravan and himself, driving a sledge with a large, strong reindeer, at the head. The rest of us then sat down on our sledges, settling ourselves with our legs stretched out in front—and off we went. Our Lapland adventure had begun.

Karesuando, the village that we were leaving, faded from view with astonishing rapidity, and soon we were out in open, snow-covered country where the whole world, as far as the eye could see in all directions, was dazzlingly white. The only variations were the shades of whiteness, of the snow, the ice, and the frost, and the occasional dark outline of stunted bare trees and low shrubs. As the reindeer clip-clopped along, relentlessly dragging the bouncing sledge up and down over the uneven terrain, I began to wish that I had a foam rubber cushion beneath me instead of hard planks covered by a reindeer skin.

But I soon forgot my discomfort in the immensity of the scene that surrounded us. We crossed one frozen lake after another that day, lakes that seemed to be silently waiting, waiting perhaps to thaw, miles and miles from anywhere, and the only sounds that cut the keen air were those we made as we crossed. And once we had moved on, the lakes would be immersed again in their total whiteness and their total silence.

In such surroundings it was impossible to be unaware that we were traversing an age-old, unmarked route that the Lapps have followed for centuries, employing the same age-old means of transport. The men use no maps or compasses but guide themselves—today as always—by means of the mountains and the lakes, for these, to the Lapps, are signposts they have known since childhood, when their parents took them along the old routes and explained how to get from one village to another—or even from one far-flung tent to another. Obviously, in a land where within an hour the weather can change from clear sunshine and blue skies to a raging blizzard, and where to get lost might well mean swift death, such lessons must be learned early—or not at all. Lapland is a hard, stern country to live in, but over the centuries its people have learned to cope with it. Now, crossing the frozen lakes, I felt a deep sense of the impressive continuity of human life, as though eternity itself were unfolding before me as our sledges jostled onward.

This land of the Lapps is, nevertheless, a land of variety, ranging from the craggy mountains of the Kebnekaise range (the highest in Sweden), with countless mountain lakes, some of which remain frozen for the greater part of the year, to the deep, dark forests lower down. The land stretches from about 62° N to 71° N, but here in Lapland it is not so much the latitude that makes for differences in climate as the height above sea level. The fixed-dwelling fisher Lapps, who live along the Arctic coast and by the low-lying lakes, and the fixed-dwelling forest Lapps of southern Lapland have quite different climatic conditions to contend with from the mountain-Lapps of the north. Is there some reason why these latter, who live closest to Nature at her most rigorous, where she exacts their utmost if they are to survive, let alone thrive, have best kept alive the traditions of their ancestors—in particular, the proud ways of the nomad? It is a question that fascinated me that day on the frozen lakes, and one I hope some time to find the answer to.

Our only change in rhythm our first day was provided by several coffee breaks. Whenever he felt like it, Aslak Utsi brought the caravan to a halt, and then he and Elsa would set about the task of lighting a fire. They would choose a spot where the snow was soft enough to be pushed and scraped away; for this purpose they would use their knives. Every Lapp—man, woman, and child—wears one of these knives in a leather scabbard hanging from his belt, and he makes use of it innumerable times during the day. Scraping aside, as now, the soft snow, shaving the bark from some birch twigs to serve as kindling, cutting up bread and pieces of reindeer meat, repairing a broken halter, branding a new calf: all these tasks are performed with this same knife.

Soon the coffee in its black kettle was ready, and though it tasted oddly bitter, it was more than welcome to all of us, for the strangers among us were unused to such extreme cold, which seeped inexorably through all the layers and layers of clothing we were wearing. Speaking for myself, I wore four pairs of trousers plus three pullovers and a thick anorak, as well as two pairs each of socks and gloves, but still the cold seeped through, partly no doubt because of the inactivity of sitting stretched out on the sledge. Our coffee breaks provided a hot drink and a welcome chance to move our legs and stamp our feet in an effort to restore our circulation.

Lapps customarily drink a tremendous lot of very strong coffee: in their tents the kettle is never very far from the fire stones, and in their fixed dwellings it sits permanently on the stove. Coffee is their hospitality drink when friends arrive; it is the first thing they want when they return from keeping watch over their herds and the last thing they partake of before setting out again; and it is their chief source of cheer and warm comfort when out on a cold journey.

1. *The snowy wilds* of Lapland provide a striking background for this Lapp and his reindeer.

2–3. *A study in contrasts:* pictured above is Kautokeino at Eastertide, blanketed in snow; opposite is the same village in summer, after the snow has melted, the river no longer frozen.

4. *A reindeer herd* crossing a strait on its way to the coastal region; the leaders have already reached land, while the main body of the herd is still in the water behind them.

5. *The northern lights* are among Lapland's more spectacular sights; glimmering faintly in the sky above is the waning

6–8. *Tents* are customary summer dwellings for Lapp families who follow the migrations of the reindeer; the poles on the opposite page have been left by a departing family for use the following year; on the right is the tent's smoke hole; below, the tent in autumn before it is dismantled.

9. *A solitary church* in the wilderness provides spiritual comfort for Lapps, fervent Laestadians, who live in tents nearby during the summer.

10. *Families* who together form a *sita* live in adjoining huts made of peat; beautiful Kvaenangen may be seen in the background.

27

11.   *A Lapp mother* with her children in front of their tent, wearing their everyday working clothes, which are sparely ornamented; the time of year is summer.

12-13. *Inside the tent:* the girl opposite is hard at work, using an old-fashioned sewing machine, while a mother, below, sitting on a reindeer skin, is peeling bark from a birch log to use as kindling.

14. *A migrating herd* is usually tended by two herdsmen, each with his own dog that has been specially trained to help keep the reindeer in order.

15. *Herdsmen in a boat* are pulling the lead reindeer into the icy water, while other helpers on shore shout and wave cloths to induce the rest of the herd to follow.

16. *Reindeer skins* are draped around wood outhouses to dry in the sun; as the weather is warm, the man has taken off his tunic and is wearing only a pullover.

17. *Autumn* is the mating season, when the fully antlered bucks fight one another to establish dominance and get to the cows first; some of the antlers are bright red.

18-19. *Roundup* takes place at the same season; opposite above, a buck is being lassoed, much against his will; below, slaughtered animals are hung up on poles after they have been skinned.

21.   *A young contestant* in Kautokeino's famous reindeer race is about to lead his entry to the starting point.

20.   *Two boys* from Kautokeino, with their reindeer and sledge, stop for a chat in the snow before continuing on their way.

22. *An admiring crowd,* on the bridge and below it, watch one of the racers drive his reindeer to the finishing line.

23. *A woman racer* tries to keep her sledge from being entangled with another that has lost its driver.

24. *Training* a reluctant reindeer to pull a sledge requires great patience and skill.

25. *Two men* from Kautokeino, one wearing a brown reindeer-skin coat with red cloth inserts.

26. *The weak winter sun* is about to set on this lonely voyager crossing Lapland's barren white wilderness.

Before evening we crossed over from Finnish Lapland to Norwegian Lapland: the fact was made known to us by marking posts, for there is no formal boundary. Somewhat later we reached the place where we were to spend the night—a *fjell-stua* (hut): small, uninhabited, and primitive, the property of the Norwegian government. In wild, lonely territories, where there are no occupied dwellings, a few of these huts are put up for the use of occasional travelers who need a roof for the night. This they provide, as well as a few bunks, a stove, and some cooking utensils, and nowhere else in the world are such basic items so deeply appreciated. The huts offer shelter, warmth, and a chance to recuperate somewhat from the trials and exertions of the past day before preparing to tackle those of the next. Under the circumstances, one can hardly expect them to provide real comfort: it is wonderful that they are there at all.

The key to the hut was over the door, waiting to be needed. We untied our rucksacks and carried them in, and once inside immediately set about getting a fire going. As for Aslak and Elsa, they still had the reindeer to tend to: the animals had to be unharnessed and then taken to a place where they would be able to find the special lichen that is their winter source of food. Although this lichen lies buried under the snow, the reindeer can smell it, and if the snow is not too hard they kick it away with their splayed feet (not, as some think, with their antlers) until they reach the juicy plants below. This was not to be found in the immediate vicinity of the hut, but the Lapps knew from past experience where there was plenty of it, and off they took the reindeer on a two-mile hike. Walking that extra distance, there and back, on top of an exhausting day, seemed to offer no challenge at all to these sturdy people.

By the time they got back, we had the stove burning, and there was already a friendly warmth in the one big room. Its furnishings could not have been simpler—double-decker bunks (eight in all), a table, and two benches—but we were well content. The soup pot was already bubbling on the stove. For water we had, of course, used snow, being careful (as Elsa had told us) to brush away the top layer, which is often acrid in taste and not suitable for cooking, and to use the softer snow beneath. We were also heating the sausages we had brought along, which were a most easily packed and easily heated food.

While we ate, Aslak and Elsa chose to sit on a reindeer skin on the floor, near the stove, rather than on one of the benches. This I found to be true of most Lapps. They prefer the floor to chairs, and they often sit back on their haunches or with one foot underneath them. They also sleep on the floor, on nothing but the hard boards—a feat I have often envied but never yet succeeded in duplicating.

Now for the first time, as we sat about eating, I had a chance to quietly study their features. Both Lapps were short, Aslak being only about five feet tall and his sister about four inches less. But both seemed quite well proportioned except for their legs, which were definitely short and rather bandy, giving them the somewhat odd gait I observed when I first saw Aslak in the clearing. This gait was less pronounced in Elsa than in her brother.

He had slanting brown eyes, rather like those of the Samoyeds or the Mongols, but his face, with its prominent cheekbones, did not at all resemble the flat Mongol type. Elsa's eyes were less slanted than her brother's and were blue; there was a touch of Scandinavian about her.

Anthropologists say that there are two distinct Lapp races, with various tribes in each race. Southern Lapps usually have a markedly triangular face, high skulls, and a blood type that shows a very low degree of allele "q"—only about four percent. Among Northern Lapps, the triangular face is altogether absent, being replaced by Samoyed or Mongolian traits, low skulls, and a blood type that shows a contrastingly high percentage of "q"—between fifteen to eighteen percent.

Basing their judgment on these and other factors, Lappologists have come to the conclusion that, as a result of early migrations in different directions, both races have to a certain extent been influenced by intermarriage with such neighboring peoples as the Finns and the Karelians as well as, further back, the Cheremis and the Mordvins. There has also been some intermarriage with Scandinavians, but to a far lesser degree, for the Scandinavians have always been averse to matrimonial connection with the Lapps.

As I came to know the people better, I grew more and more fascinated by the visible differences between them, and intrigued by the realization that many Lapps today are taller and stronger than those of only a generation ago, as well as by the fact that some are remarkably more Scandinavian-looking, even though they too may be true nomads.

After we had finished our meal, we made some more of that eternal coffee, and I now began to understand why everybody in our group had brought at least one whole package of coffee with him. I had thought, when we set out, that this was rather an excessive amount for a three-day journey, but now I saw that when we reached the end of it, there would very likely not be a bean left.

We were all tired after that exhausting day, and so, one by one, we soon began to peel off a few outer layers of clothing and then crept wearily into our sleeping bags, still wearing the rest of our clothes. I, finding my bunk not only rock-hard but lumpy as well, and considering the prodigious quantity of coffee I had drunk, lay there convinced I would probably not sleep a wink all night. . . . And that was the last thought I remember. When I woke it was morning, and the coffee routine was by then well under way again. What, I wondered, as I pulled one sweater over another, would a staunch, tea-drinking Englishman make of this crash course in coffee appreciation that we were getting?

When breakfast was over, Elsa gave us a demonstration of the Lapp art of stuffing reindeer-skin shoes with warm, dry grass. These shoes, called *skaller*, are, with their turned-up toes, the best footwear to use on dry snow. Inside the shoes the Lapps do not wear socks but rather an insulation of dried sedge grass, which they shape around the foot. They collect this grass in the summer, the finest and softest they can find, and then prepare it by first combing it and afterwards beating handfuls of it against a rock to soften it still further. Once they are satisfied with its texture, they twist it into plaits and then wind the plaits together in big round bundles to keep for use in winter.

Elsa now, as we watched, took one of these bundles from her sledge, along with extra *skaller* that she had with her, and she offered to lend us these and show us how to pack the grass around our feet. She did it with such facility that we all decided we would have no difficulty copying her. After having untied the plait, she rubbed and kneaded it gently into an almost rectangular pad, and then she put it down as she waited patiently for us to catch up with her. Finally, she folded it around her right fist and pushed it into her shoe. Obviously it needed to be just thick enough to leave room for the foot and to be smoothed out on all sides to a uniform thickness. Simple enough, we all thought as we followed suit, but the results were so odd that Elsa was seized with uncontrollable hilarity. Some of us had put so much grass in the *skaller* that there was no room left for the foot, while others had a tremendous lump of grass on one side and nothing at all on the other. I managed to get both my feet into the *skaller* and also to surround them with grass; the only hitch was that the grass beneath the soles of my feet was of such varying thicknesses I could walk only with the most outrageous limp!

Lapps, of course, become accustomed to the use of this sedge-grass almost from the moment their lives begin, for their cradles are lined with it. These cradles are remarkable objects, by the way, made of hollowed-out birch logs with a birch hood, and the whole thing covered with leather. Down the length of the cradle, on either side, is a row of loops, through which a thong is threaded to hold the leather cover in place and so prevent the baby from falling out. The softest sedge-grass available is used to line the cradle, and when it gets wet or soiled it is discarded and replaced with fresh grass to keep the baby warm. This simple, highly effective system was in use long before disposable diapers.

Aslak Utsi had gone off to collect the reindeer and to harness them for the day's drive, and while he was away we cleaned up the hut and sawed some wood to replace what we had used. We felt no sense of hurry, for we knew that even with the help of his two trained dogs Aslak would be quite some time preparing the reindeer.

Happily, time is not money in Lapland. Indeed, Lapps seem to have no sense of time at all—nor any need of one. I soon discovered how pointless it was to try to arrange to do anything with a Lapp on a specific day at a specific time, for although *I* used to be there as arranged, *he* certainly was not, and this failure was not the result of any rudeness or ill will. It is just that time—as expressed in hours, days, or even weeks—has very little meaning for a Lapp; for him it is the seasons that count, and that is how he reckons time.

In winter Lapland has two months of total darkness, darkness that lasts twenty-four hours a day, every day. The sun remains below the horizon, and the only light that nature provides is intermittent moonlight and an occasional display of northern lights. Summer is the opposite: there are two months of constant daylight, when the sun never sets at all, and the whole land is bathed in the soft, golden glow of the midnight sun. Century after century the Lapps have lived with these two extreme conditions. They do not, consequently, divide time into units of twenty-four hours, as we do, but rather into far longer units: "the dark time," "the light time," and "the time between," for any job that can be done on a summer day can just as well be done on a summer night. Thus, the Lapps eat, sleep, and work to this seemingly irregular pattern that is fashioned by the necessities of the seasons and the moment, not by any daily rhythm.

Several hours after we started out on our second day's journey, we suddenly caught sight of something moving in the distance. It was the first life we had seen since leaving Karesuando, and we all were very curious about what it might be. As we approached a little nearer, we could see that it was a lone reindeer—and a very young one.

Pulling the caravan to a halt about fifty yards away from the reindeer, Aslak spoke briefly to Elsa, then picked up his lasso, slipped his skis on, and started to walk towards the calf. Elsa meanwhile explained to us that sometimes, when a herd of reindeer is migrating back to the mountains in the autumn, one of the young gets separated from the rest and left behind. Since calves are born the preceding May, so young an animal has very little chance of surviving the winter alone, unaccustomed to finding nourishment for itself, and at the mercy of wolves and bears.

If the owner of a herd notices that a calf has strayed, he will do everything he can to find the animal, but he cannot hold up the autumn migration of several thousand reindeer in order to search for one. So it sometimes happens that a calf has to fend for itself through the winter, without the protection of the rest of the herd and the herdsmen.

Since the time of year was now March, this particular calf appeared to have managed, but it was evidently weakened, for it allowed Aslak to approach within about ten yards before it started to run. By that time Aslak had his lasso ready, and its coils flew swiftly through the air, landing neatly and precisely over the young reindeer's head.

"It's not one of ours," said Elsa, "but we will tie it to the back of my sledge, and if it survives the journey to Kautokeino, we'll return it to its owner."

How, I wondered, could she tell at fifty yards' distance whose herd the reindeer belonged to? This ability, I was to discover, is one of the most extraordinary gifts of the Lapps. At that distance, neither I nor any of the Scandinavians could even tell whether the little reindeer had a brand in its ear or not. But Elsa could not only see the brand, she could tell whose mark it was.

Every Lapp reindeer owner has a brand of his own, which is registered by law, and each of his calves is branded with this mark as soon as the owner finds it, usually some time in summer or autumn.

49

LAPLAND

The calf always stays close to its mother (who is, of course, already branded), so ownership is easy to establish. Nomadic Lapps know by heart all the brands of reindeer owners in their own district and in adjacent districts, and so keen is the eyesight of these nomadic people they can recognize the brand at well over fifty yards.

Elsa gave the calf some of the dried lichen that she had in her sledge, and then tied it to the back. Aslak meanwhile had already kicked off his skis. This he did far more quickly than he could have done if they had been Alpine skis, for the only attachment is a loop of leather in the front, into which the turned-up toe of the Lapp shoe fits. Then he put his single, very long ski pole back on the sledge, and we were once again on our way. Added now to the interest of the journey was our gnawing uncertainty whether the little reindeer—"our" reindeer—would make it all the way back to Kautokeino, where he might be restored to his owner.

The loss of a reindeer can be a serious matter to the owner of a Lapp herd, for the animals are often his only means of making a living. His ability and success are judged by the extent to which his herd increases over the years, and his wealth is reckoned by the number of animals that, at any given moment, bear his brand. Perhaps that is why it is considered impolite to ask a Lapp how many reindeer he owns—just as it would be impolite in most parts of the world to ask a man how much money he has in the bank.

As we journeyed on, Aslak's two dogs ran up and down the length of the caravan, moving much faster than the reindeer, which frequently sank into the heavy snow. A Lapp dog (a breed of Spitz) accompanies his master everywhere, even sleeping at his feet in the small tent that he takes with him when he is away tending the herd. The dogs are of enormous help to him in rounding up the reindeer and in keeping them from straying once they have been rounded up. During the big spring and autumn migrations, the dogs play an indispensable role: if reindeer stray, the dogs pursue them and drive them back to the herd; at the same time, they urge on the lazy deer at the rear of the herd.

A big herd of migrating reindeer moves in the shape of a triangle. At its head is a Lapp herder (who walks or uses skis, depending on the season), leading—by means of a rope—a buck that has a bell around its neck. Close behind comes a buck that has been trained to follow the first without being led by anybody; this is the most valuable animal in the entire herd because it is he that sets the example for the other reindeer. After him there comes a small troup of tame bucks and does—the elite of the herd, so to speak— also with bells around their necks. Then, fanning out to the rear, moves the main body of the herd, driven by their instinct to follow the leader, and driven also by a desire to follow the sound of the bells, which to them signals the security of the herd. The base of this vast moving triangle consists of reindeer that are lazy or stubborn or that have no native or acquired desire to follow the leader. It is these animals that tend to stray off and get lost, eventually falling prey to one or another of the perils of winter. It is the job of the dogs to prevent their doing so.

Just as the light began to fade that evening, we passed a hillock on top of which, outlined darkly above us, stood a huge, curiously shaped rock. I found out afterwards that this was an ancient *seida*—a rock sacred to the Lapps of long ago. These people believed that an oddly shaped or strangely placed rock had special powers over the region where it was found—and that they could ask the rock to use these powers on their behalf. The people might make offerings to the rock—reindeer antlers, for instance, or bowls and spoons carved from antlers—and ask the rock in return to help them find the wild reindeer they were hunting. Sometimes an entire Lapp community made offerings to a special rock, but more often the rock was considered sacred to one particular family.

This primitive form of worship was gradually replaced by Christianity, beginning around the thirteenth century, but the Lapps were not really converted until the coming of Thomas von Westen, a Norwegian clergyman who was responsible also for the conversion of the Swedish Lapps, and who is, in fact, known as "the Apostle of the Lapps."

Then, in the nineteenth century, a new and strange form of revivalism arose, which has persisted to the present day. It took its name—Laestadianism—from one of the most unusual personalities in the history of the Scandinavian church, Lars Levi Laestadius. He was born in the year 1800 in Arjeplog to a family of poor Swedish Lapps, and it was only with great difficulty that he acquired sufficient schooling to become a minister. This he did at the age of twenty-five, beginning his ministry in the northernmost part of Swedish Lapland, where he was destined to spend the rest of his days.

He soon decided that the Lapps' worst enemy was alcohol, which had been introduced to them by the Bir-karls and to which they had taken with such enthusiasm that among the poorer Lapps its effect was paralyzing. Overindulgence was common among both men and women, and (as a result, perhaps) there was much immorality. The religious war that Laestadius mounted against these evils was characterized by such fervent preaching on his part that it caught the imagination of the Lapps as nothing else had since their pagan days; and the revival that he began spread across the borders from Swedish Lapland to both Norway and Finland. Even today it continues to play an important role in the life of the Lapps: religious meetings frequently culminate in a kind of religious ecstasy, where everyone confesses his sins at the same time, where the whole congregation embraces one another, and where each grants all others forgiveness for their sins.

That night the waning moon, which had been covered by clouds the night before, shone clear and cold. The frost-covered twigs of the low birch trees glistened and gleamed in its light, and the shadows of the reindeer and the sledges danced weirdly on the snow. In an effort to stay a bit warmer, most of us were walking beside our sledges; in places where the snow was dry we raised a powder so fine it looked almost like steam or vapor in the moonlight; and as we walked, I turned frequently to watch this.

It was very late when we got to bed that night in a hut that, to my tired eyes and in the dim light, looked exactly like the one we had slept in the night before. It was not until the next morning that I discovered how different it was, for part of it was permanently inhabited by a Lapp family who kept their reindeer nearby during part of the year and who (a fact that was of more interest to us) were willing to provide hot food for hungry travelers.

The men of the family were seminomads, following their reindeer during the migrations, then taking turns living at the hut in between these trips. The women helped with the slaughtering and other tasks, and were also, as I soon discovered, remarkably proficient at Lapp handicrafts. They made not only all their own clothing (as all Lapp women do) but also shoes and gloves of reindeer skin, which they sold to travelers who stopped at the hut.

They also had what may best be described as small hand looms ("weavers' reeds"), on which they wove beautiful bands of blue, yellow, and red yarn. These long, narrow bands are used as shoe-laces and are also wound round and round the top of a shoe at the ankle to hold it fast to the trouser leg and so help keep out the cold. Belts can also be woven on these looms—but the Kautokeino Lapps, men and women both, generally wear leather belts that are heavily decorated with brass buttons and plates.

That morning, as I wandered about, I stopped for a time to look at the small rescued reindeer, who was lying down near the hut with some dried lichen in front of him. He looked very tired indeed; and I, not knowing how far we still were from Kautokeino, wondered uneasily whether he would survive the journey. Not only the calf but all of us seemed to be feeling tired that morning, and lazy too, after our two days of strenuous travel, and it was well into the afternoon before we got started again.

When Aslak told us that the temperature had dropped to minus 27 °C. during the night, I was not surprised that we had felt a chill as we walked in the moonlight. In deepest winter it gets even colder: minus 46 °C. has been registered at Kautokeino and minus 51 °C. at Karasjok. Average winter temperatures, however, are not so extreme—minus 11 °C. in December, minus 14 °C. in January, and minus 12 °C. in February. Summer temperatures are much higher than might be expected, averaging 12 °C. in June, 16 °C. in July, and 14 °C. in August. Summer extremes registered at Kautokeino and Karasjok are 29 °C. and 32 °C. respectively.

♒ THE JOURNEY

We had been traveling for some time on that third day when we encountered a Lapp skiing in the opposite direction, toward the hut where we had spent the night. His approach was the signal for us to pause and bring out the coffee kettle. Lapps, when they are on a journey, love to meet one of their own kind, for it is usually someone whom they have not seen for a long time, and so they settle down happily, squatting on their haunches in the snow, drinking their coffee and gossiping, squinting their eyes against the smoke from the fire.

As I listened to the gossip, I thought how strange the language sounded. It belongs to the Finno-Ugric family of languages, which is, in turn, related to the Samoyed. Finnish and Hungarian are the best known of the Finno-Ugric group, while other, lesser-known tongues are the Vogul and Ostyak of northwest Siberia and a number of languages in the eastern and northern parts of European Russia. Of all this group, Lapp most closely resembles Finnish in cadence, but the vocabularies are too far apart for Finns and Lapps to understand each other. And within the Lapp language itself there are so many different dialects, each totally unlike the others, that Lapps have a language problem among themselves: a Lapp from Jaemtland, for example, can not understand a Lapp from Karesuando—although both these places are in Swedish Lapland.

Over the centuries during which the Lapps have been in contact with their non-Lapp neighbors, they have come to realize the need to be familiar with these languages too, and most Lapps speak the language of the country they live in, while many also know the tongues spoken in bordering countries. It is not at all uncommon to meet a Lapp who speaks Finnish and Swedish or Norwegian in addition to his own language.

LAPLAND 🦌

Young Lapps of today, who have better opportunities than ever before for advanced schooling, often learn English as well, and then later perhaps some German and even French. There are good modern schools in both Kautokeino and Karasjok, as well as in Jokkmokk and Gaellivare in Sweden, where all the usual subjects are taught in addition to the history of the Lapp people themselves. Whether or not the students plan to go on to a university, they are required to remain at school until they are fifteen.

There are also folkcraft schools, where Lapp girls are taught to make the beautiful clothes they wear, to weave, and to embroider in the ancient manner with pewter thread. Boys learn to carve objects from reindeer horn and to decorate them with the same beautiful designs that their ancestors used—geometrical patterns and conventionalized flowers.

For the latter, there is always a plentiful supply of raw material, since both male and female reindeer grow antlers which fall off and are renewed every year. Males shed theirs in autumn, after the mating season; females in early summer, after they have calved. Thus males still have their antlers when they need them to fight off rivals during the mating season, and females still have theirs when they need them to defend their young.

Our own little calf seemed to be growing weaker, collapsing immediately onto the snow every time we made a stop, but whenever we moved on again, he somehow struggled up and stumbled along after us. As I watched him on one of these occasions, I suddenly realized why Aslak and Elsa were so anxious to save him: his fur was snow-white, a fact that, in the eyes of the Lapps, made him especially valuable, since most reindeer are grayish beige, although they change color somewhat from season to season.

The reindeer-skin coats that the Lapps wear for warmth on everyday occasions are made of these grayish beige skins, but when a Lapp wants a special coat for a special occasion, then one made entirely of the rare white skins is indicated—and indeed a pretty Lapp girl in a pure white reindeer-skin coat is a very lovely sight indeed. After white, black skins, which are also very rare, are the next most valuable, then brown, and at the bottom of the list the common grayish beige.

That third day, as we traveled onward, it seemed to grow dark very early, perhaps because we had made such a late start. But Aslak comforted us with the words: "We'll reach Kautokeino in a few hours."

As darkness fell, northern lights gradually became more and more clearly visible, hanging over the horizon in front of us, shimmering in long, pale blue streaks. For some time they seemed to stay more or less in the same place; then, even as I watched, they suddenly darted across the sky, undulating like a living thing as they went, adding and changing colors all the time.

The phenomenon was soundless of course—a circumstance that should need no comment except that I found the silence odd, for I somehow subconsciously associated the northern lights with lightning, which brings thunder in its wake. But the northern lights have nothing to do with lightning, nor are they dangerous, though ancient Lapps used to be afraid of them, and their folklore frequently speaks of them as a force that might kill anyone who mocked them.

But if the northern lights are silent, what—I wondered—was

that strange clamor that suddenly rent the evening air? It was Aslak. Stimulated by the nearness of Kautokeino and by all the things he was looking forward to doing there, and excited by the strangeness of the northern lights, he had abruptly broken out in a loud *joik* (which is the Lapp way of singing). This is one of the most primitive forms of musical expression existing anywhere on earth today, and someone hearing it for the first time may be pardoned for being startled—or even alarmed out of his wits. Its audible effect is overwhelming and I find that trying to capture this effect in words presents both a difficult and compelling challenge.

The *joik* is a form of song with a short repeated text, often improvised, and punctuated with meaningless sounds in between, such as *voya, voya* or *nana, nana*. It rises and falls according to the intensity of feeling of the singer; it continues for as long as he or she feels inclined; and it ends quite abruptly in what often sounds to outsiders like the middle of a word.

Most *joiks* are either atmospheric descriptions of places and events or else characterizations of people, according to their physical appearance, and peculiarities, such as the shapes of their noses or their ways of walking. Every Lapp village has its own descriptive *joik*, and so also—among the reindeer-Lapps—has every individual. Some *joiks* are satirical, others are frankly erotic. This latter quality has led fervant Laestadians to regard the *joik* as sinful, especially since most Lapps will not *joik* until drink has relaxed their inhibitions somewhat. Thus, the *joik* and alcohol have become commonly associated.

But Aslak, untroubled by such considerations, was happily filling the night with what must have been the Kautokeino *joik*:

♪ THE JOURNEY

> Kautokeino, *voya, voya*!
> Village where there's blood on the knife!

This presumably is a reference to the infamous massacre at Kautokeino in 1852. The Kautokeino Lapps sing a *joik* also about the village of Karasjok, which is, of course, not the same *joik* that the Karasjok Lapps sing about themselves. The Kautokeino version goes something like this:

> Karasjok!
> Village of dullards and dimwits!

This would suggest something about the nature of the relationship between the two settlements.

We were now driving down the frozen river of Kautokeino; then a sharp bend in the riverbank brought the Lapp village suddenly into view: a few lights here and there in the darkness, some of them isolated, others in clusters, the dim outlines of houses and other buildings, a church spire.

At this point Elsa joined the *joik*:

> Kautokeino!
> *Nana, nana!*
> Kautokeino!

And thus in a burst of frenzied song we drew up in the center of the village, under the bridge that spans the river. We had made it!

And so, I was relieved to discover, had the little reindeer. He looked pitifully thin, and when we came to a stop his legs collapsed under him again, but I no longer felt anxious on his behalf: now he would be able to rest and eat until he was strong enough to rejoin his herd.

We all felt similar needs for eating and resting, needs we satisfied in short order in a modest but comfortable guest house; here we enjoyed the delights of the first hot water and real beds that we had seen since Karesuando.

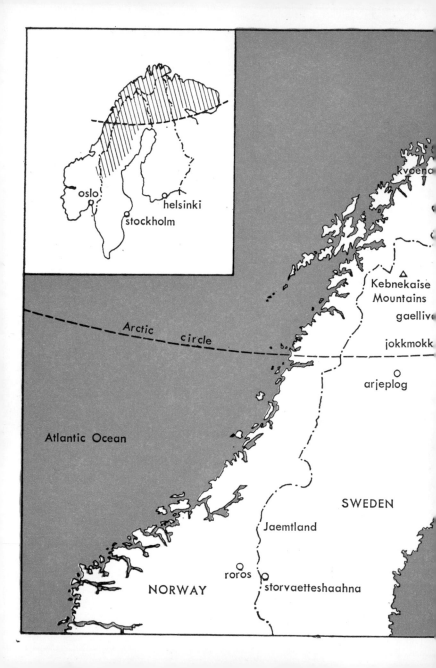

ARK
Okarasjok
keino

esuando

Kola Peninsula

tnian

ulf

RUSSIA

FINLAND

THE VILLAGE

Sightseeing, the next day, in this Lapp village in the wilds of Finnmark, I noted first of all that its houses were simple wooden dwellings, similar in appearance to those found in other north-Norwegian, non-Lapp communities. The people who own and live in these houses of Kautokeino are Lapps who have given up full nomadism in order to become either seminomadic or to take up some other form of livelihood altogether, such as running a little grocery shop or cultivating a small plot of land. The majority of the people are the seminomads—those who follow the reindeer on the big migrations but who return to live in Kautokeino in between. With some families only the herdsmen go with the reindeer, while the women and children remain at home.

Apart from the dwellings and shops, there were a few small cafes, two schools, a church, a hospital, a hotel, and a few small guest houses, but the overall appearance of the village was rather dull. Far from dull, however, were the colorful figures walking up and down its streets, for this was Eastertide, the time, above all others, when Lapps of different tribes come together at Kautokeino, not only to celebrate the feast but also to meet and exchange gossip (which remains one of their favorite pastimes), to attend the weddings that take place every year at this season, and to buy provisions for the coming spring migrations with their herds.

The costumes of the Kautokeino tribes are the most gorgeous to be seen anywhere in Lapland, and of course the majority of the people we saw were proudly wearing the costumes of the tribe to which they belonged, though some of them lived quite far from the village.

Both men and women wear a bright blue tunic of woven cloth, the women's of dress length, the men's shorter. The tunics are extraordinarily full, sewn as they are with so many inserts, and they are decorated over the back and shoulders, as well as at the hem, cuffs, and neck, with wide, colored bands of bright red, yellow, and green.

Both men and women, again, use ornate leather belts, some of which are decorated with two rows of studs pierced through the leather, with round brass buttons between. These belts make the tunics puff out below the waist; women's tunics, especially, swing widely from side to side with every move of the wearer.

There being no pockets in the tunics, Lapp men have evolved a highly satisfactory alternative: they wear their belts low, sometimes around the hips, and use the upper part of the tunic as a kind of huge pouch in which they store everything they think they are likely to need, such as pipe and tobacco, drinking cup, and the like. It is not at all unusual to see a Lapp who has just made some purchases in a shop put them down the front of his tunic and walk off, oddly bulging here and there perhaps, but with his hands free.

Under their tunics, women as well as men wear narrow, reindeer-skin trousers. Their shoes also are of reindeer skin, and in summer they wear leather boots with turned-up points. In winter everyone in Lapland wears a heavy reindeer-skin coat over his usual tunic.

The hats of the men are made of stiff pieces of cloth, about a foot high and decorated with same colored bands as their tunics, sometimes with inserts of reindeer fur. From the top falls a floppy piece of blue cloth with four points, also decorated with four bands. On festive occasions they fasten colored streamers, a good yard long, to the sides of their hats. Women's caps are of bright red cloth, pouched at the back and decorated with colored bands. The women also sport a bright silk or woolen scarf over their shoulders and fastened in front with a silver brooch.

The Kautokeino Lapps wear these lovely costumes nearly all the time. In the spring the women make new costumes for the whole family, which are kept for special occasions, while last year's clothes are used for everyday wear.

Here and there, I noted as I walked through Kautokeino, were Lapps from Karasjok who had found their way to the rival village. It was easy to pick them out from the majority, for their costumes were much more sober. The tunics were dark blue, not bright blue, and the cut of the women's tunics was longer and more sedate than that of the women of Kautokeino. Being narrower, these Karasjok tunics did not swing enticingly from side to side but hung rather limply, like sacks. The drab effect was increased by the fact that the women often do not use belts, nor do they sport so many colored bands. The women's caps too, though red, are smaller and not so highly decorated.

Much the same is true of the men, whose clothes do not compare in elaborateness with those of the Kautokeino men. Most interesting, I found, were the hats, which have at the base a wide band of cloth (in summer) or reindeer skin (in winter), and are topped by blue

27. *A Lapp wedding* is a highly ceremonial affair: here the bride's mother is fastening the wedding sash under the groom's belt, with a brooch in front.

28. *The bride,* wearing a veil over her pouched red cap, is being decorated with the many rings that a Lapp bride wears at her wedding.

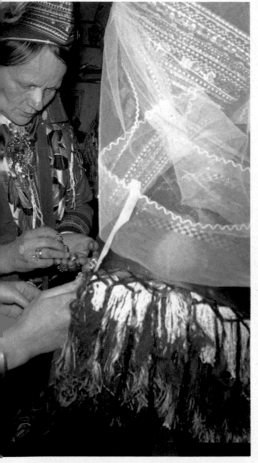

29. *The wedding procession* leaves the bride's home to make its way to the church; the couple themselves, in the middle of the procession, are hidden from view.

30. *Inside the church,* the bride and groom are seated in front of the black-robed pastor; standing at his right is the Lapp interpreter.

31-32. *After the ceremony,* the newly-weds stand on the church steps to be admired, then another procession escorts them back to the house for the wedding "breakfast."

33. *Wedding guests,* in a never-ending stream, partake of reindeer meat specialties and other dishes; everyone is invited, and the more people that come the better are the chances for a happy marriage.

34. *The feast* may go on for as long as three or four days and nights. And after the feast comes the washing-up—but there are plenty of willing hands to help cope with the mountain of dishes.

35-37. *Three young ladies* show the diversity of racial types among the Lapps. On the left is a girl from the Finnish side of Karesuando; on the right, a typical Lapp from Kautokeino; and below, another girl from Kautokeino wearing her everyday summer clothes.

41-42. *A Karesuando woman* proudly shows off her lace-edged cap, while a woman from Kautokeino (below) poses with her little grand-daughter.

43–44. *This Karasjok cap* is clearly an old one, for the peaks have lost their stiffness; below are two men of the Karesuando tribe, one wearing the typically gigantic red pompom.

45. *A very old Lapp woman* sports a costume of her own invention and contentedly smokes a pipe; she keeps her tobacco in the reindeer-skin pouch beside her.

cloth in the shape of four high, stiffened points filled with sedge grass to make them stand up in four directions. The points symbolize the Four Winds far more effectively than do those of the Kautokeino hats, which are floppy rather than stiff.

I decided that the Lapps of Karasjok had been more deeply influenced by their Laestadian religion, which frowns on all luxury and ostentation, and that their costumes reflected this attitude. Further, though both villages are in Norway, the Lapps of Karasjok are very different from the Lapps of Kautokeino in their methods of reindeer herding as well as in many other ways, including their way of thinking.

More closely related to the latter are the Lapps of Karesuando, and there is frequent intermarriage between the two. The men of Karesuando wear close-fitting cloth caps, with a leather peak, decorated with colored bands and surmounted by an enormous bright red pompon. Women's caps are also close-fitting; they are made of red cloth, with a few narrow bands and a ruche of white lace that frames the face. The Lapps of Jokkmokk wear clothes that are almost as sober as those of the people of Karasjok, but the Jokkmokk cap has the same bright red pompon as that of Karesuando.

Karesuando has the perhaps unique distinction of lying in two different countries, for part of it is in Sweden and part in Finland. On the Swedish side it boasts a church and a few cafes; the houses are much like those of Kautokeino. Between the two halves of Karesuando runs a river; in the winter it is frozen and so permits the villagers to walk from one part to the other; in the summer there is a small ferryboat.

LAPLAND

Most of the Lapps we encountered that first morning in Kautokeino seemed to be heading in the same direction, and when we inquired, we discovered that this was the day of the big reindeer race and everyone was going to watch it. We went along.

The racecourse was near the bridge, not far from where we had ended our journey the night before, and was a simple track, up one side of the frozen river and down the other, which had been flattened out to make the going easier. Normally reindeer do not run very fast, they prefer to plod steadily rather than to move swiftly, so racing them is no easy matter. Considerable preliminary training is required to persuade a reindeer to actually run while it is pulling a sledge and a man.

This race is held every year at the same time and is one of Kautokeino's major Easter attractions. There may be as many as a hundred competing drivers—men, women, and children—each of whom is given a large painted number to wear over his clothes. The contestants start one at a time, with a few minutes' interval between. Each leads his animal and sledge up to the starting point, and at the signal leaps onto his sledge and begins to beat his single rein up and down rapidly on the flanks of his reindeer, at the same time giving out the most blood-curdling yells.

This combination is supposed to extract the maximum speed from the reindeer, and if the driver is lucky, he may even finish the race. But if he is unlucky, any number of things may go wrong. During the race we watched, one young Lapp was tipped out of his sledge three times; yet each time he managed to hang onto the rein and to climb back. One reindeer, altogether ignoring both the race course and his driver's efforts to make him follow it, headed straight off down river. Another was so slow and lazy that the following reindeer caught up with it, and the two sledges, despite frantic efforts to get them apart, became inextricably tangled. They finished the course together in a slow zig-zag, accompanied by a furious argument between the two drivers as to whose fault it all was. The high degree of excitement is understandable if one bears in mind that reindeer racing is virtually the Lapp's only sport; skiing—to the Lapp—is a means of transport rather than a sport.

At the race that day the best time was made by a woman driver, but this apparent ignominy did not seem to embarrass the men at all. The Lapp way of life is very definitely not a matriarchy, and yet women have always held a privileged place in Lapp society. The daughter of reindeer-owning parents, for example, is given a herd of her own, just as her brothers are, and she has her own brand.

A Lapp child is presented with his first reindeer when he cuts his first tooth; then other reindeer follow to mark other significant days, such as birthdays, his first day at school, confirmation, and so on. By the time a Lapp boy or girl is grown, he or she has a sizable herd of his own, which forms a separate unit within the large family herd.

The girls, who are as good as the boys at tending the animals, also help with the fishing and other tasks that are often held to be male prerogatives in other societies. A married woman has her own special place in the family tent, a place that is hers by inviolable right, and her opinion carries weight on any subject that comes up for family discussion. She has a decisive say in all economic consultations, and the final say when it comes to accepting or rejecting a marriage partner for one of the children.

LAPLAND

Weddings in Kautokeino are just as exciting as reindeer races, and that same day there were several of them. Before a young couple actually reach that decisive moment, however, they may have had to undergo a number of ordeals. This is especially true for the groom, since Lapp parents, who are extremely difficult to please when it comes to finding spouses for their children, are particularly choosy about daughters.

One reason is that a girl takes her herd of reindeer with her when she marries, along with the other animals that her father gives her to mark the occasion. This means the loss of an important number of animals for the bride's family, and a major gain for the fortunate groom. Another reason involves the loss of the girl herself and the contribution she makes to the well-being of the family, such as helping to tend the herd during a migration (especially important if the herd is a large one), making clothes for the family, and so on. Thus, a suitor has no light task, for he must be accepted not only by the girl herself but also by her parents.

Customarily, Lapp girls have a number of suitors, a fact that gives them and their parents time to make up their minds. To demonstrate the seriousness of their intentions, these suitors give the girl presents, depending on their means: silk scarves and silver brooches are the most popular gifts. She is permitted to accept them from any number of suitors, so if one sees an unmarried girl wearing a large number of lovely brooches, one has no doubts about her popularity. Once, however, she has definitely decided on a particular man, the rejected suitors are entitled to ask for their gifts back—with no hard feelings.

A girl accepts a suitor only after her parents have given their approval; no Lapp girl would marry a man her parents did not approve of. So once a girl has indicated her favorite, it is up to him to prove to her parents that he is the right husband for her. For this he needs his entire family to back him up; when he goes to make his formal proposal, he takes with him his father, mother, brothers, sisters, grandparents, and any other close relations he can muster.

During the entire negotiation (for such it may indeed be termed), the prospective groom leaves all the talking to the one who has been chosen "head of the wooing." First, the whole expedition arrives at the tent or house of the girl's parents, suitably armed with brandy and other ingredients for a celebration. They ask permission to enter and to distribute the refreshment they have brought; if permission is granted, this is taken to be definite encouragement in the business at hand.

Everyone being comfortably settled, the two sides get down to bargaining. The economic loss in reindeer and labor that the departure of the girl will mean to her parents and the corresponding gain to the family of the prospective groom must be compensated for in some way. Thus, in the bargaining that takes place at this official meeting, the girl's parents try to make the compensation as high as possible, while the boy's parents try to keep it as low as possible.

The negotiations follow a customary pattern. The "head of the wooing" praises the hopeful suitor in glowing terms, pointing out his ability as a reindeer breeder, the immense size of his herd, and the like. It is then up to an elder member of the girl's family to make disparaging remarks about the boy, denigrating his economic position, his skill with reindeer, even his personal character. The "head of the wooing" then refutes these disparaging remarks and perhaps makes a counterattack against the girl. The prospective bride and groom sit in absolute silence throughout the negotiations no matter what may be said, leaving it to their elders to thrash the matter out.

Eventually some agreement is reached as to what presents, including perhaps money, the suitor must give the parents of the girl to compensate them for the loss of their daughter and also how many reindeer and how much in the way of household goods the parents will in turn give to help start the new family off. Nearly always, one term of the bargain provides that the young couple shall live with the bride's parents for the first year and that during this time the husband will help tend the reindeer and assist in other ways. Once all the provisions of the contract have been formally agreed to, the couple are considered engaged, an event that is now celebrated by all attending members of both families.

The couples who were to be wed at Kautokeino that Eastertide all came from places some distance away from a church, so once they had become engaged they had had to wait to marry until Easter, when the necessity to buy provisions for the spring migration brought them to the Lapp village.

Promptly at twelve noon, as the church bells pealed across the still air, the first bridal procession emerged from a house at the end of the village. Pairs of girls and boys escorted the bridal couple, who walked in their midst, to the church. There they were joined by parents and relations, and the whole party moved inside, followed by most of the population of Kautokeino as well as many people from distant parts.

Bride and groom seated themselves on chairs in front of the altar, and before them stood a soberly dressed pastor, looking very drab in long black robes and white ruffed collar. The pastor conducted the marriage service in Norwegian, and it was translated, sentence by sentence, into Lapp by the pastor's assistant, who stood nearby. It was very short: some twenty minutes later the young couple, now man and wife, were once again outside the church, standing hand in hand on the steps, surrounded by their families.

The bride was splendidly arrayed. She wore *two* of those beautiful Kautokeino dresses, one on top of the other, which swayed in thick folds as she moved and made her waist look very small. She also wore not one or two but *four* silk scarves, arranged one over the other across her back in such a way that all their different fringes were displayed in tiers. In front she had affixed a dazzling assortment of beautiful silver and gold brooches: if these were all gifts from her husband, he must, indeed, have been a man of means. Over her red cap she wore a veil, and in her hand she carried a bouquet. The flowers, I was somewhat surprised to see, were artificial. The groom wore his very best costume and over his shoulders sported a white bridal sash, crossed in front.

As they paused for a time in front of the church, friends came up to congratulate them, and then the whole party proceeded sedately back to the house they had come from—to celebrate the wedding in true Lapp style. By evening the entire village was filled with the sounds of revelry (including some wild *joiks*), for everyone was in a festive mood and was determined to make the most of these few short days when they could be together with friends and relations whom they might not see again for many months.

My Norwegian friend and I were lucky enough to be invited to the home of one of the newlyweds, where we watched the proceedings with undisguised fascination. In one room long tables had been set up, at which a steady stream of guests sat down, eating their fill before making room for another shift.

The more guests that come to a wedding party, the Lapps believe, the better are the chances that the young couple will have a happy marriage: everyone in the village, therefore, is welcome at these celebrations. As they continue for some three days and nights, people have plenty of time to attend all the wedding parties that may be taking place at the same time. Not infrequently there are as many as four hundred guests at a house where a wedding is being celebrated.

The main dish, called *bidos*, is a kind of stew made of the choicest cuts of reindeer meat and both smells and tastes delicious. It is served with plain boiled potatoes and flatbread. Then come stewed prunes, the usual strong coffee, and a special cream-filled cake, which the Kautokeino baker has produced for the occasion. Once everyone has eaten, strong drink begins to go the rounds and is drunk straight from the bottle; after a time, the *joiks* seem to increase in variety and intensity. This, by the way, appears to be the only form of Lapp social activity: the people have no dances of their own, nor do they dance at social gatherings.

In some of the cafes of Kautokeino, Karesuando, and elsewhere, today's omnipresent jukebox may be found, and the young people eagerly feed it coins to extract the tunes it contains—but they only sit and listen to the music; they do not get up and dance.

Even the games that the children play are not like those of other peoples but are rather games intimately related to the Lapp way of life. Indeed, sometimes they are not mere games at all but a kind of training for abilities that will be needed later. One such is, in fact, a favorite: it consists of several children holding reindeer antlers above their heads and running around in a counterclockwise direction (as reindeer do at the time of the separation of the herds in autumn) while the other children try to lasso the antlers.

Then there are bear games, in one of which a sleeping child "bear" plays the main role, while in another the children act out the killing of a bear and the bringing home of the body. In fact, the ceremonial hunting of the bear, along with the many superstitions and beliefs that attend to it, plays a dominant role in Lapp history and legend.

The games I have mentioned are all played outdoors, but Lapp children have indoor games as well. One is the reindeer-herd game, in which two children, usually squatting on their haunches opposite one another, hold in the space between them a flat, slightly hollowed-out piece of wood about a foot wide and two feet long. On this wooden tray each player "owns" a number of fir cones, each cone representing a reindeer. Large old fir cones are male reindeer, new cones are does, and small ones calves. Each contestant shakes the tray in turn, making the cones jump from one side to the other. As he does so, the child cries, "Look what a lot of your reindeer have come over to *my* herd!"

In these and other ways the Lapps reveal that, although for centuries they have had constant contact with the very different Scandinavians, their culture and way of life have remained very much their own—in the far north of Lapland, at any rate. Today there is even a daily program in Lapp on the Norwegian radio, and both newspapers and magazines are published in the Lapp language. Almost every Lapp family, incidentally, owns a radio, and transistors are an absolute boon to the nomads because now, no matter where they are, they can hear weather predictions, which are broadcast four times a day. Obviously, nomadic Lapps are far more dependant on the vagaries of the weather than are many more sedentary Scandinavians, and hearing about expected changes can be extremely helpful to them.

LAPLAND ♂

One striking example of how Lapp culture differs from most others is that their rules of inheritance are based on the right of ultimogeniture, that is to say, it is the youngest son, not the eldest, who inherits the family house or tent as well as any other property, including the father's reindeer brand. In return, it is the youngest son's duty to stay at home and take care of his parents as long as they live and also to provide for any unmarried sisters. This rule is still very much in force in Finnmark.

Nowadays there are homes for old people, and some Lapps, if they become feeble and chronically ill, do go into them; but many still prefer to live with their families and—so long as they are able—to take part in the annual migrations. To accompany the reindeer, sometimes for several hundred miles and often in bad weather conditions, perhaps in heavy snow and perhaps going without sleep for forty-eight hours at a stretch, is hard and grueling work, but it is also a source of great joy to the nomads, as the age-old rhythm of the herds renews itself once again. And the elderly feel that, somehow or other, so long as they can make that migration, cost them what it will, they are still in the mainstream of the way of life of their people.

A Lapp poem, called "Gadja's Journey," tells of an old, old man named Gadja who had become so infirm that he had to give up his nomadic way of life and stay in one place, living in a house where people could look after him. But this new way of living was so foreign to him that in the end, longing for his old life, he cries out in despair:

> My sleep must be slept where the herds are—
> In our own valleys;

Only there where I understand what the living are doing,
Can I grasp what the dead are saying.
I can get no rest in this fixed dwelling,
With its "John, you must come here at once."
I hear the barking of our herd dogs—
And I know that my time is nigh.

True nomads have always looked down on those who live in fixed dwellings, and they still do, for it is the reindeer owners who are the aristocrats of their race. The sedentary ones are presumed to be those who could not—or whose ancestors could not—make a success of reindeer husbandry, and who therefore had to look elsewhere to earn a living.

Perhaps no other animal in the world has so shaped the way of life of a whole people as the reindeer has shaped the destiny of the Lapps. Ever since the Lapps of long ago made the wild reindeer herds their own, their descendants have had to bend and mold their lives to conform to the reindeers' needs.

By far the most important of these is the need to migrate twice yearly, chiefly in search of varied nutrition. During the winter the reindeer find too little of the rich lichens that they have eaten all autumn and that now lie buried under the snow. This is particularly true if the ground itself is frozen. Nor can the deer move very far in search of food, because the deep snow hinders and tires them. They must manage as best they can on the far less nourishing beard lichens and crust lichens, and by the end of winter they are often quite thin.

LAPLAND 🦌

Then at last, in early spring, the snow begins to melt and a crust starts to form on its surface. As soon as this crust becomes thick enough to bear the weight of a reindeer, the herd starts to move down from the mountains to summer pasture regions near the coast, where there is a plentiful supply of tender grass and herbs.

Almost as soon as the herd arrives, the does begin to calve. The little animals roam with their mothers all summer and by autumn they, like their parents, are fat and strong—strong enough to withstand the coming winter.

The mating season occurs in autumn. By this time the coastal grass and herbs have withered, so the reindeer start to move again, eating the good, rich lichen as they go back to the mountains where they will be able to find at least some kind of lichen on which to survive the winter. In this way too they manage to avoid the millions (this figure is not an exaggeration) of mosquitoes, midges, and gadflies that would torment them all summer long if they remained in the mountains.

Winter and summer, then, are relatively quiet seasons for Lapp reindeer owners; their periods of peak activity are spring and autumn, when they must try to organize the migrations as best they can. This means (among other things) that they must pack everything they are likely to need onto sledges and that they must have their best draft reindeer constantly ready to pull the sledges. They themselves will most likely have to walk, for the herd must be watched and kept together both by day and by night. Herders will almost certainly have to cover at least two hundred miles over difficult terrain in snow conditions that may change from hard crust to deep slush, and with the ever-present possibility of a dense fog or a sudden snowstorm.

The does are instinctively anxious to accomplish the great trek to the coast before they drop their calves in May, for newborn deer could not possibly walk so far so fast. Some years the snow is slow to melt, and as a result the necessary top crust forms late; under such conditions it may be May before the migration can begin. Then both the animals and their owners are filled with such a sense of urgency that they keep going twenty-four hours a day for days at a time. The needs of the men for sleep and food are subordinated to the overwhelming need of the deer to reach the coast as soon as possible.

Once they arrive, the herders put up their tents or else move into peat huts, which they may have built the summer before, or even earlier, and which will serve as their summer homes. These rough huts are usually cone shaped, like the tents the ancient Lapps first dwelt in, and usually have a wide smoke-hole at the top, just as tents have, although some huts are roofed and use an iron stove instead of an open fire. In either case, the huts are made of birch and are covered with birchbark and peat—a fact that makes them darker inside than a tent.

The tents, built over a framework of birch poles, are made of sacking in summer and of thick woolen material in winter. The two pieces of material of which they are constructed are fastened together at the pole opposite the entrance; the entrance itself is a triangular piece of sacking, stiffened by wooden slats, which can be easily pushed aside from within or without. At the top is an opening about four feet across to let out the smoke of the fire below. The floor is covered with birch twigs, which are frequently renewed, and in the center is a ring of fire stones.

The family bedding (reindeer skins and woolen rugs) is stacked around the inner edges of the tent, so as to be out of the way during the daytime. Each member of a Lapp family has his or her set place for sitting or lying—a place decided by ancient custom; it may be on the right or left side of the fire stones, or at the back of the tent or near the entrance. The mother of the family has the best place of all, at the back, where the tent is warmest. The worst place is near the entrance, which may be full of smoke from the draft, and this often falls to the hired herdsmen who share the family tent.

Each member of the family also has his or her allotted share of work. Men do the hunting and most of the herding; women prepare skins and sew clothes. Women also cook most of the food, although there is an old custom, which still persists, that says it must be the husband, not the wife, who cooks the meat from an animal that has just been slaughtered. This custom dates back to the taboos of the first Lapp hunters.

Once the Lapps and their herds have reached the summer pasture grounds, both are able to take things easier for the next few months. While the animals feed, their owners fish in the sea and the lakes, drying part of their catch for use in winter; they cut sedge grass and prepare it; and they gather wild berries.

There is daylight the whole time. Frequently the children are up in the middle of what we would call the night, playing in the soft light of the midnight sun.

But the short summer of Lapland is over all too soon, and the coming of autumn means rounding up all the reindeer (which may be spread out over a considerable area), separating them into herds according to their brands, and slaughtering enough of them to fill the needs of the various families. All this is a tremendous task, to accomplish which the owner of each herd needs all the help he can get, not only from grown sons and hired hands but also from womenfolk and children.

Frequently a group of families living near each other migrate together, in a *sita*. As each member of every family has his or her own individual herd, there can be as many as twenty herds that have roamed together all summer and that now have to be separated so that calves can be counted and if necessary branded, and so the total number of reindeer in each herd can be reckoned. Only in that way can the owner tell whether any deer are missing and whether his herd is prospering.

There is yet another consideration: every owner wants to be reasonably certain that other owners are not slaughtering any of *his* reindeer. At all stages of breeding, two very powerful influences play upon the Lapp herd owner: the first is his primordial desire to increase his herd by every available means (which is accompanied, of course, by a corresponding dislike of doing anything that may decrease the herd, such as slaughtering some of the animals). The second is a deeply rooted conviction that, although the animals with his brand are undoubtedly his, the ownership of deer with other brands is not nearly so certain.

This confusion is not altogether the fault of the modern-day herd owner; it dates back to ancient times when mountain Lapps first began to hunt wild reindeer. Even after they managed to form them into herds, they continued to regard the deer as semiwild animals, of which nobody had absolute ownership. They were the collective property of the tribal community; thus no member of the tribe who took a communal reindeer could ever be accused of stealing, for he was only taking something that belonged to him as much as it did to anyone else.

LAPLAND ⚓

Among mountain Lapps this attitude persists to some degree today. Anyone who thinks he can get away with it will blithely brand any young calves he comes across with his own mark even though its mother is plainly branded otherwise. And if he finds a small group of reindeer that have strayed from the main herd, he will cheerfully "look after" them for the real owner; and should his "looking after" remain undetected, he will just as cheerfully slaughter them for his family's needs, leaving his own herd undiminished.

Although the Lapps are an honest people, they somehow believe that anything to do with the breeding and keeping of reindeer lies beyond the realm of honesty or dishonesty; they believe that any action can be justified. Having discovered this, I began to wonder whether Aslak Utsi took all that trouble getting the lost calf back to its rightful owner because of a scrupulous sense of honesty, or because there were so many pairs of eyes watching him when he found it.

In this respect the forest Lapps of the southern regions differ markedly from those of the mountains to the north. The former have now, and have always had, a more restricted form of reindeer husbandry; nor are they so dependent upon it for their livelihood. Throughout history they have owned fewer animals, and they have not owned them tribally, like the mountain Lapps, but individually. This fact obviously led them to take sterner views on the delicate question of "stealing" reindeer.

These two Lapp peoples differ also in other ways, such as their methods of lassoing their reindeer. Mountain Lapps, who have plenty of space around them in which to swing their lassos through the air, drop the loop over the reindeer's antlers. Southern forest

Lapps, on the other hand, often had to lasso their animals in places thick with birch trees, in the branches of which a loop might easily snag, so they developed a technique of swinging the lasso low and catching the reindeer by the feet.

It is no easy task to capture reindeer by either method, for they put up tremendous resistance, kicking and bucking in all directions, so much so that it often takes two men to hold one reindeer down. But a Lapp is intensely proud of his abilities with reindeer and he will not always accept help.

This is, in fact, a delicate question, almost one of prestige. If the animal is to be slaughtered for the family's needs, then the family will accept help from whoever happens to be on the job with them. But if the animal is being lassoed for some other purpose (perhaps merely in order to be belled), then the man who is trying to catch it will likely be too proud to accept assistance. Even if he is battling against a big, strong, recalcitrant buck, he will probably prefer being pulled off his feet, dragged along the ground (still clutching the lasso), and having his clothes torn in the process, if in the end he can boast that he has subdued the turbulent reindeer alone and unaided. In this way his prestige among his fellow Lapps will have been considerably enhanced.

On the question of the relationship between the mountain Lapps and their reindeer, little has changed in the many years since 1648, when Johannes Tornaeus wrote a book called *Manuale Lapponicum*, in which he has beautifully depicted this symbiotic association:

It is impossible fully to describe what a useful and noble animal the reindeer is. For from the reindeer the Lapp has his food and his clothes, his conveyance and his sustenance, and many household articles. While it lives, it gives the Lapp both milk and cheese—and moreover it is not only quite handy for transport, but also swift enough on journeys.

And yet the Lapp is not bound to incur any expenses for it; it needs neither any stable in winter, nor forage; wherever it comes to by nightfall, it sleeps under the open sky—and it finds its food for itself.

When it is slaughtered there is nothing to be found in it which is not useful. First, the meat is not only eatable, but it is as fat, good, and savory as any meat can be. In the bones there is excellent marrow, of which the Lapps make such a feast as we make of oysters or some early fruit. From the skin they get fur coats—from the leg-skin and the head-skin they get leggings, shoes, and gloves—as well as harnesses and what else may be needed for straps and the like. They use the sinews instead of thread—not only for clothes but also to seam together their boats and boat-shaped sledges. With the hides they do their best trading and pay their taxes. Out of the bones and horns they make scoops, spoons, and all kinds of other household goods.

In short, to the Lapp the reindeer is more valuable and useful than any other animal is to any people on the earth!"

And this all remains true of those Lapps who still gain their livelihoods almost entirely from their reindeer herds. It is sad to report, however, that the number of these Lapps is slowly shrinking, growing smaller year by year. Sometimes their children, living at school in Kautokeino or Karasjok and rejoining their parents in the family tent only during holidays, become so accustomed to the non-nomadic life that they choose some form of sedentary work after they leave school.

Others, who want nothing more than to carry on the age-old traditions of nomadism and reindeer husbandry, find that the basic conditions that permit this kind of life grow more and more restricted. The reindeer still roam in search of food, to be sure, but not so freely as they once did. And Scandinavian farmers now have rights over land that once belonged to the Lapps alone. Further, industry is being encouraged to move north, and some areas have been taken over by mining developments.

All this means progress to the Scandinavians, but for the Lapps it can only be interpreted as regress. They are a minority in their own land; their pasture grounds, both winter and summer, shrink each year; every reindeer owner is now alloted a set, limited range for his herd. His animals may not, as they used to, go further in search of nourishment should it happen to be a bad year for reindeer food in his allotted region. And each range, even in a good year, will provide food for only a limited number of animals—a fact that prevents the owner from enlarging his herd, thus going against all his deepest instincts and his proudest traditions.

The Lapland of northern Norway is today the last stronghold of the true Lapp way of life. How long it will continue to be so is, I suppose, anybody's guess. Certainly I would not hazard one. But I shall come back from time to time to see—for I have become a *Lappin hulu*, which is the Lapp name for a person who, having been to Lapland and having fallen under its unique spell, feels the gnawing need to return.

46. *Father and son,* both blessed with hearty appetites, tuck into their noonday meal.

103

47. *Social life* is limited but satisfactory: here, over a couple of beers, two Lapps catch up on a year's gossip and compare notes about the forthcoming winter's snow.

48. *A jukebox* in Lapland is only for listening: nobody in this small Kautokeino cafe would think of getting up to dance in public.

49. *This elderly woman* wanted a copy of h[er] picture but was unab[le] to write down h[er] address: her daught[er,] who had been [to] school, came to t[he] rescue.

50. *Darts* were a new experience to these Kautokeino Lapps, visiting a Scandinavian friend on the coast near their summer tents; but they soon became experts.

51. *Lazily watching* the reindeer in summertime, this herdsman whittles a walking stick for himself.

52. *A traveling salesman,* having set up his stall outside Kautokeino's Monix Cafe, attracts an eager horde of village children.

107

53. *Mikkel Bongo* plays a simple instrument (that he himself invented) on Lapp radio programs——and as he plays, he *joiks*.

54. *Odd Haetta*, another well-known Lapp radio personality, gathers his material on the spot and then broadcasts it to the Lapp world.

55. *Weighed down* with skis, rucksack, reindeer skins, and food pouch, this elderly Lapp is relieved to be nearing his tent.

56. *A typical sledge* has iron runners both fore and aft of the seat; a second person may stand on the rear runners and give a push from time to time.

57. *Bicycles* are also a favored means of transportation with the Lapps.

59. *This blue truck* brought distant guests to a wedding in Kautokeino one year when the snow was very bad for sleighing and the rough mud track was the only way to reach the village.

58. *Three Kautokeino women,* when asked to pose for a photograph, grew desperately shy and began to giggle among themselves—but they did not turn away from the camera as the picture was snapped.

60. *Sacred rocks,* called *seide,* were believed by ancient Lapps to have the power to grant favor and protection if properly propitiated.

61. *A rock painting,* over four thousand years old, shows a magician beating a magic drum while another figure, probably a woman, dances to its rhythm.

63.   *A weaver's reed* shown at an exhi
bition of work done by pupils at th
Kautokeino Handicrafts School.

62.   *A Lapp nomad* is depicted on a
stained-glass window in a church in
the far north of Norway.

64. *Reindeer horn* carved into paper knives and needle holders.

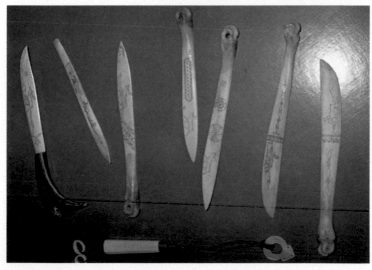

119

65. *A little Lapp girl,* thoughtfully sucking her finger as she stares into the camera's eye, is wearing a costume designed (and of course made) by her mother.

66-67. *A Lapp cradle* is constructed of hollowed birch covered with thin leather and decorated with woven bands; it is lined with soft sedge grass and has a hood to protect the baby's head. In the photograph below, the hood has been removed and the baby is seen playing with his older sister.

68. *Lapp children,* very
fond of animals, are
shown here romping
happily with a little
kitten.

123

69-70. *Reindeer calves* often become family pets, when they are born too late or are not strong enough to make the long, exhausting spring migration with the rest of the herd.

71. *In this schoolroom* at Kautokeino, the teacher—a Norwegian from Oslo —spoke no Lapp, so the younger children, unused to hearing any language but their own, had great difficulty understanding her at first.

72. *Children* who come from places too far from Kautokeino to go home daily live at the school during the term.

73. *Tree-climbing* is a favorite pastime with boys all over the world, and Lapps are no exception, as this little boy from Kautokeino demonstrates.

74. *A boy plays* with his tricycle outside the family tent, which is pitched in summer beside a road where the family sells homemade souvenirs to passing tourists.

75. *These children* are waiting for a bus that will take them and their belongings to Alta, a small town on the coast, where they can buy provisions.

76. *Having no choice* but to make her journey on foot, this Lapp mother carries her baby in a rucksack strapped to her back.

77. *A cloth-covered board* serves as a stand where the family displays the reindeer-skin shoes it has made to sell to travelers —but the curious little boy has appropriated the stand.

78. *Wearing her best costume,* this Kautokeino girl sits in the snow, just as she has seen her parents do.

◀79. *Gaily dressed,* a pretty little girl from Kautokeino smiles happily at the photographer.

80. *A field of buttercups* makes an attractive background for this young Lapp girl; the scene is typical of the coastal regions of Norwegian Lapland.